A

DOMESTIC COOK BOOK

CONTAINING

A CAREFUL SELECTION

OF USEFUL RECEIPTS

FOR THE KITCHEN

A

DOMESTIC
COOK BOOK:

CONTAINING

A CAREFUL SELECTION OF USEFUL RECEIPTS

FOR THE KITCHEN.

BY

MRS. MALINDA RUSSELL,
AN EXPERIENCED COOK.

PUBLISHED BY THE AUTHOR.

PRINTED BY T. O. WARD, AT THE "TRUE NORTHERNER" OFFICE,
PAW PAW, MICH.
1866.

A DOMESTIC COOK BOOK

CONTAINING

a

CAREFUL SELECTION

of

USEFUL RECEIPTS

for

THE KITCHEN

MALINDA RUSSELL

University of Michigan Press
Ann Arbor

For questions or permissions, please contact
um.press.perms@umich.edu

Published in the United States of America by the
University of Michigan Press
Manufactured in the United States of America
Printed on acid-free paper
First published February 2025

A CIP catalog record for this book is available from the British Library.

Library of Congress Cataloging-in-Publication data has been applied for.

ISBN 978-0-472-03964-7 (paper : alk. paper)
ISBN 978-0-472-90435-8 (open access ebook)

DOI: https://doi.org/10.3998/mpub.12837641

The University of Michigan Press's open access publishing program
is made possible thanks to additional funding from the University
of Michigan Office of the Provost and the generous support of
contributing libraries.

CONTENTS

CONTENTS

viii

CONTENTS

Digital materials related to this title can be found on
the Fulcrum platform via the following citable URL:
https://doi.org/10.3998/mpub.12837641

CONTENTS

Both recipes and specific ingredients in this cookbook should be viewed in historical context, particularly with respect to the small number of toiletries and cures that appear near the end of the book. Ingredients such as lead and laudanum were commonplace in the 19th century but can be highly dangerous and should not be used today. Similarly, certain herbs and plant products can be toxic and even non-toxic herbs can cause allergic reactions or interact badly with conventional drugs.

JANICE BLUESTEIN

LONGONE:

A LEGACY TO SAVOR

BY

Juli McLoone

THE ONLY KNOWN ORIGINAL COPY of Malinda Russell's 1866 *A Domestic Cook Book*, the oldest known published cookbook written by an African American woman, now makes its home in the University of Michigan Library's Special Collections Research Center. This important book is a part of the Janice Bluestein Longone Culinary Archive (JBLCA), a rich collection of cookbooks, menus, advertising ephemera, and other assorted culinary materials, with a focus on documenting American foodways from the 18th–20th centuries. This collection had its origin in the early 2000s, when Janice Bluestein Longone and Daniel T. Longone began donating their personal collection—amassed over decades—to the University of Michigan. You can read Jan Longone's story of finding Malinda Russell's fragile but powerful volume in Jan's own words, in the introduction to the 2007 facsimile edition, reprinted in this edition of *A Domestic Cook Book.*

Before Malinda Russell's *A Domestic Cook Book* surfaced, the oldest known published cookbook written by an African American woman was *What Mrs. Fisher Knows About Old Southern Cooking*, written by Abby Fisher and first published in 1881. In reading Russell's cookbook, Jan Longone recognized its importance as a work that predates Mrs. Fisher's by over a decade, as a collection of recipes that adds nuance to our understanding of what constituted 19th-century African American cuisine, and as the story of an indomitable woman. Most of all, though, Jan recognized that this was a book that should be treasured by being shared. In a 2019 interview with public radio station WEMU, Jan explained that while she had prepared some of the recipes in the cook-

book, she was ultimately more interested in get-
ting other people to try making them.[1] Jan wanted
Malinda Russell's recipes and story to be known
and appreciated as a crucial thread in the tapestry
of American culinary history. This desire was made
manifest by the publication of a limited facsimile edition in 2007 for a culinary symposium held by the
William L. Clements Library, and by the digitization
of both the original and facsimile editions by the University Library in 2016.[2]

Jan's interest in the history of food production,
preparation, and consumption goes back to her days
in graduate school at Cornell University, where she
studied Chinese and Indian history. In an anecdote
she shared often, Jan and her husband Daniel T.
Longone, who studied organic chemistry at Cornell and went on to be a Professor of Chemistry at
University of Michigan, were often hosted by fel-
low students sharing foods from their respective
homelands. When asked to reciprocate with a "typical American meal," Jan realized what complicated
questions that simple phrase engendered.[3] Investi-

gating those questions led Jan on a rich journey over subsequent decades, from a lifetime subscription to *Gourmet* magazine, to a quest to collect a Jewish charity cookbook from each of the 50 states for the exhibit "American Foodways: The Jewish Contribution, 1660–2013" co-curated with Avery Robinson.[4] In the 1970s, Jan began publicly sharing her passion for all things culinary by hosting *Adventures in Gastronomy* on public radio station WUOM. Through her antiquarian bookshop in Ann Arbor, The Wine and Food Library, Jan came to know many luminaries of the 20th-century culinary world; Julia Child, M.F.K. Fisher, Jeremiah Tower, and James Beard were among the many who came to rely on Jan as a source for esoteric and unusual cookbooks.

As broader academic and societal interest in food history and culture developed in the 1980s and 1990s, Jan was at the forefront. She was a founding member of the American Institute of Wine & Food; wrote "Notes on Vintage Volumes," an occasional column highlighting various aspects of culinary history through rare cookbooks for the quarterly journal

Gastronomica; gave lectures at the Oxford Food Symposium on Food and Cookery; and served as a judge for organizations including the Tabasco Community Cookbook Awards and the James Beard Foundation. Together, Jan and Dan co-founded the Culinary Historians of Ann Arbor and Jan served as honorary president of this vibrant group for many years.

In 1999, Jan, who had previously served as an informal advisor for food history acquisitions at the William L. Clements Library, took on more formal responsibilities as Curator of American Culinary History, working to expand the University's culinary history holdings and encourage this increasingly popular area of study.[5] In 2001, Jan and Dan Longone donated Malinda Russell's *A Domestic Cook Book* to the University of Michigan. Soon after, the Janice Bluestein Longone Culinary Archive was established, and the Longones began donating their personal collection of cookbooks, menus, and other culinary history documents to the University of Michigan. The Archive was initially housed at the William L. Clements Library, and in 2013, moved to the University

Library's Special Collections Research Center.

Jan was the recipient of many awards recognizing her crucial role in developing the discipline of food history, among them the Food Arts Silver Spoon (2000), the Amelia Award for Lifetime Achievement in Culinary History (2011), and the Carol DeMasters Service to Food Journalism Award (2018). The accolades that meant the most to her, though, were the relationships she developed and maintained with students and researchers who came to her for guidance and whose interests she was able to support and develop through the years.

In 2005, Clements Library Director John C. Dann expressed a hope that the Janice Bluestein Longone Culinary Archive, then in its infancy, would encourage others to adopt what he described as Jan and Dan's own "enthusiasm and limitless curiosity" in investigating the history of food and drink.[6] We in the University of Michigan Library are now pleased to continue this legacy by providing access to the historical record of American culinary history through the Janice Bluestein Longone Culinary Archive, and by encouraging that same enthusiasm and curiosity in future generations of scholars, cooks, and scholarly cooks.

Notes

1. Jorge Avellan, "Hidden In Plain Sight: Oldest Known Cookbook Authored By An African-American," WEMU 89.1, April 15, 2019. https://www.wemu.org/wemu-news/2019-04-15/hidden-in-plain-sight-oldest-known-cookbook-authored-by-an-african-american

2. The original edition can be viewed at https://hdl.handle.net/2027/mdp.39015091768104. The facsimile edition can be viewed at https://hdl.handle.net/2027/mdp.39015073926647.

3. Randy Schwartz, "A Pioneer of American Culinary History: Remembering Jan Longone (1933–2022). *Repast: Quarterly Publication of the Culinary Historians of Ann Arbor* 38, no. 4 (2022): 24.

4. Jan Longone, *Lecture on American Foodways: The Jewish Contribution, 1660–2013,* September 24, 2013, Hatcher Graduate Library, University of Michigan, Ann Arbor, MI, 1:06, https://leccap.engin.umich.edu/leccap/player/r/IiDsbw

5. "Announcements," *The Quarto* no. 12 (1999): 12. https://clements.umich.edu/wp-content/uploads/2019/09/quarto12-3-dimensional-objects.pdf

6. John Dann, "Please Come to the Table" *The Quarto* no. 23 (2005): 1. https://clements.umich.edu/wp-content/uploads/2019/09/quarto23-culinary.pdf

INTRODUCTION TO
THE 2007 FACSIMILE EDITION

MALINDA RUSSELL:

AN INDOMITABLE WOMAN—

AN AMERICAN STORY

BY

Janice Bluestein Longone

MALINDA RUSSELL'S *A Domestic Cook Book*, published in 1866, is a fascinating first-person chronicle of a free woman of color in mid-19th century America. Hers was a life of "hard labor" and travail, but she overcame all her hardships and setbacks with an indomitable spirit. It is truly an American story.

Like its author, the fragile copy of *A Domestic Cook Book*, housed in the Janice Bluestein Longone Culinary Archive at the Clements Library, is a survivor.[1] To our knowledge, it is the only copy extant of the first cookbook authored by an African American.

Who Was Malinda Russell?

All we know about Malinda Russell is what she tells us in "A Short History of the Author" and her "Rules and Regulations of the Kitchen." Her story, outlined below, is remarkable, and I encourage you to read her first-hand account in this facsimile.

Malinda Russell was born and raised in Washington and Green Counties, eastern Tennessee. Her mother was a member of one of the first families set free by a Mr. Noddie of Virginia. "My mother being born free after the emancipation of my grandmother, her children are by law free."

When Russell was 19 years old, she set out with others for Liberia. When her money was stolen by a member of the party, she was "obliged" to remain in Lynchburg, Virginia. There she began working as a cook and a companion, traveling with ladies as a nurse. She also kept a wash-house and advertised in a local newspaper; she included a reproduction of one such ad in her book.

While in Virginia, she married a man named Anderson Vaughan, who lived for only four years thereafter. For the rest of her life, she used her maiden name. At the time of writing *A Domestic Cook Book* (1866), she was still a widow with one child, a son who was "crippled."

At some point after her husband's death, Russell returned to Tennessee and kept a boarding house on Chuckey Mountain, Cold Springs, for three years. After leaving the boarding house, she kept a pastry shop for six years, and "by hard labor and economy, saved a considerable sum of money for the support of myself and my son."

Then, for the second time in Russell's life a robbery forced a change in her existence. On January 16, 1864, her money was stolen from her by a guerilla party, who threatened her life if she revealed who they were. "Under those circumstances, we were obliged to leave home, following a flag of truce out of the Southern borders, being attacked several times by the enemy." After "hearing that Michigan was the Garden of the west," she moved to the Paw Paw area "for the present, until peace is restored, when I think of returning to Greenville, Tennessee, to try to recover at least a part of my property."

The Genesis of *A Domestic Cook Book*

Russell was employed as a cook for the last 20 years of her life by the first families of Tennessee, Virginia, North Carolina, and Kentucky. She learned her trade, she tells us, from Fanny Steward, a colored cook of Virginia, and she cooked after the plan of the "Virginia Housewife." This last is most likely a reference to Mary Randolph's classic and very popular work, *The Virginia House-wife*, first published in 1824. It had at least 19 printings before the Civil War and is still in print.

Forced to leave the South because of her Union principles, Russell wrote her book "hoping to receive enough from the sale of it to enable me to return home." Now "advanced in age," robbed of her property, and with no means of support other than her own labor, she decided to write a cookbook "with the intention of benefiting the public as well as myself."

Russell ended her brief autobiography with the confident assurance that "I know my book will sell well where I have cooked, and am sure that those using my receipts will be well satisfied."

Perhaps because of Russell's diverse background and varied travels, the "receipts" in her book are not distinctly southern. Nor do they appear to have been taken from Mrs. Randolph's *The Virginia House-wife*. We have not been able to learn anything about Fanny Steward, the Virginia cook Russell mentions.

Most of the recipes could come from any part of the eastern United States of that period, although there are a few southern touches, such as "Sweet Potato Baked Pudding," "Sweet Potato Slice Pie," and "Fricaseed Catfish." Most recipes are for sweets, desserts, and baked goods, not surprising given Russell's years of keeping a pastry shop. For this facsimile we have added an index of the approximately 265 recipes and medical and household hints in the cookbook to make it easier for modern culinary historians to use.

Discovering Malinda Russell

It is quite astonishing that this unique copy of *A Domestic Cook Book* has survived. I do not know how many hands it passed through between its printing in 1866 and our purchase of it and subsequent donation to the Clements Library several years ago. The book was found at the bottom of a box of material from the collection of Helen Evans Brown, a well known California culinary figure in the last half of the 20th century. Her bookplate appears on a modern protective paper cover enclosing the book.

When my husband Dan and I received a call from someone on the West Coast wanting to know what we knew about *A Domestic Cook Book* by Malinda Russell, we answered honestly that we knew nothing about it—not even that it existed. But we very much wanted to purchase it. Fortunately, we were able to do so. When the book arrived, we were stunned at what it represented—an important and previously unknown piece of American culinary history.

Determined to discover more about Malinda Russell from the few tantalizing details she revealed in her "Short History," Dan and I spent our 48th wedding anniversary in Tennessee, Virginia, and North Carolina visiting historical societies, cemeteries, government offices, and other locales she mentions. Several times, we felt we had captured her or were very close, but in the end, we could not be certain we had unequivocally identified her from among the available documents.

Dan and I spent a great deal of time trying to solve the mystery of this remarkable woman. When we felt we could no longer devote the time necessary to collect any new information, I chose to write about Malinda Russell for an article in my "Vintage Volumes" column in the first issue of *Gastronomica* (2001). Some of the material in this introduction first appeared there.

The response to that article was a bit overwhelming; many readers wanted to know more about the author and her cookbook. Given this interest, I hoped that someone would be able to devote the time and energy required to add further information to her story, although, alas, that has not yet happened.

Malinda Russell in the Context of 19th Century Black Culinary Literature

The Clements Library's unique Malinda Russell cookbook is one of the four 19th century culinary works by African Americans that have so far come to light. Although *A Domestic Cook Book* (1866) is now considered the first cookbook written by an African American, there are two earlier manuals on household management and hotel and dining room work authored by professional Black men: Robert Roberts' *The House Servant's Directory* (1827) and Tunis Campbell's *Hotel Keepers, Head Waiters and House-keepers' Guide* (1848). The fourth book by a 19th century African American is Abby Fisher's *What Mrs. Fisher Knows About Old Southern Cooking* (1881).

The House Servant's Directory by Robert Roberts was the first book of any kind by an African American printed by a commercial publisher in America. Of major gastronomic importance, the book was published in 1827 in Boston by Monroe & Francis, with two additional printings in 1828 and 1843.

Roberts was a butler in the household of the Honorable Christopher Gore, Senator and Governor of Massachusetts. His book is remarkable for several reasons. It offers one of the most detailed discussions of that period on the proper management of a

fine, upper-class New England household. It gives
advice to servants on how to behave, how to perform
their work, and how to use the variety of new household utensils and equipment then becoming increasingly available. Although Roberts comments on the
responsibilities of the employer, he is generally more
interested in teaching other servants how to act.

His work is one of the first to help encourage
young Black men to become the finest professional
house servants. He offers specific, detailed sugges-
tions to them to ensure their advancement and ten-
ure. In addition to his influence on Black employment
patterns, Roberts was active in various organizations
promoting Black interests.

One indication of the influence of *The House Servant's Directory* is its inclusion in the library at the
Hermitage, President Andrew Jackson's home in Tennessee. One of a handful of culinary books in the Hermitage library, it shares honors with Mrs. Randolph's
The Virginia House-wife, the first southern cookbook.

Roberts' book has long been known to culinary
bibliographers, and facsimiles and reprints are avail-

able. This book is of New England; there is nothing either African American or southern about the recipes.

Tunis Campbell's *Hotel Keepers, Head Waiters and Housekeepers' Guide*, published in Boston in 1848, is known to bibliographers, but it has been little examined due to its rarity.

Born in New Jersey early in the 19th century, Campbell attended an Episcopal school in New York and was trained for missionary work in Liberia. But he became increasingly opposed to the planned removal of Black people from America to Africa, "having long since determined to plant our trees on American soil."

Between 1832 and 1845, he became a social worker, reformer, abolitionist, and an active participant in anti-slavery causes. During this time, he worked in New York as a hotel steward, the last three years as the principal waiter at the Howard Hotel. Then, for an undetermined period, he worked at the Adams House in Boston. While there he wrote his *Guide,* one of the earliest manuals written by any

American on the supervision and management of first-class restaurants and hotel dining rooms.

Campbell's book is evocative of a military manual. He gives detailed, exacting instructions, with illustrations, for the dining table service brigade. As careful as he is to instruct and train his waiters for their responsibilities, he is equally voluble in telling the employers that they also have a responsibility to treat their help with respect and dignity.

Hotel Keepers, Head Waiters and Housekeepers' Guide deserves to be better known, but only a few copies of the original exist, and, to my knowledge, there is no facsimile in print at present. Campbell is better known to American historians for his non-culinary contributions, including his many years as a powerful force in Reconstruction politics in Georgia.

Abby Fisher's *What Mrs. Fisher Knows About Old Southern Cooking* was printed in San Francisco by the Women's Co-operative Printing Office in 1881. Until the discovery of Malinda Russell's work, this book was considered the earliest Black-authored cookbook.

Mrs. Fisher was an ex-slave who could neither read nor write. Born in South Carolina, she achieved fame in San Francisco, where she had a business of pickles and preserves manufacture. Her cookery was awarded medals and diplomas at several California fairs, including two medals in San Francisco in 1880 for "best pickles and sauces and best assortment of jellies and preserves."

Mrs. Fisher's collection of recipes, with origins in the plantation kitchens of the pre-Civil War South, was published with the assistance of named benefactors in San Francisco and Oakland. Her book is perhaps the earliest California imprint of importance beyond the confines of the state. Because of its scarcity it was little known until recently, but several facsimiles have made the book more widely available.

Uncovering the shrouded origins of the first known Black cookbook in the United States is only one of the mysteries of American culinary history that remain to be solved. There are several other major questions to tempt the historically minded—books whose authors' identities and lives are hidden beyond what they themselves provide within the pages of their works.

Who, for example, was Amelia Simmons, the self-labeled "American Orphan," author of the first American cookbook (1796)? Who was Mrs. Esther Levy, "neé Esther Jacobs," author of the first Jewish cookbook in America (1871)? Or who was Mrs. W.R. Sanner, whose recipe collection is the basis of more than a dozen charity cookbooks published between 1907 and 1915 in states as diverse as Ohio, Nevada, and California? Each of these women deserves to be better known.

I am confident that making this facsimile of *A Domestic Cook Book* available to a wider public will stimulate further research that may allow that indomitable spirit, Malinda Russell, to take her rightful place at the American culinary history table.

Malinda Russell's story is an American story. She has overcome.

(2007)

Note

1. When Jan Longone wrote this introduction for the
    2007 facsimile edition, the original copy of *A Domestic
    Cook Book* resided in the William L. Clements Library.
    It now makes its home in the University Library's
    Special Collections Research Center, to which the
    entirety of the Janice Bluestein Longone Culinary
    Archive was transferred in 2013.

FOREWORD TO
THE NEW EDITION

MALINDA RUSSELL:

_____

IN THE SHADOW

_____

OF SLAVERY'S

_____

KITCHENS

BY

Rafia Zafar

ALTHOUGH AMELIA SIMMONS published the first cookbook by an American in 1796 Connecticut, it wouldn't be until the second half of the nineteenth century that recipe books written by African Americans began to appear. The earliest similar, Black-authored volumes, Robert Roberts's *The House Servant's Directory. A Monitor for Private Families* (1827) and Tunis Campbell's *Hotel Keepers, Head Waiters, and Housekeepers' Guide* (1848), are most accurately described as hospitality and housekeeping manuals—recipes for furniture polish and instructions for stoking stoves are included along with meal recipes. Not until 1866, when Malinda Russell brought out *A Domestic Cook Book: Containing a Careful Selection of Useful Receipts for the Kitchen*, would a work by an African American entirely focused on food and drink recipes appear; the volume furthermore earns pride of place as the first cookbook published by a Black woman. Russell inaugurated the tradition of Black middle class chef-author; until the publication of her book, African American cooks could not be imagined as writers. Prior to her publishing her work, there were renowned Black chefs performing masterful feats for Founding Fathers—George Washington's homes were ornamented by Hercules Posey, Thomas Jefferson's Monticello by the French-trained James Hemings—but Russell was the first African American to author a collection of recipes. Within decades, chefs like Abby Fisher, Rufus Estes, and E. T. Glover, followed.[1] But Malinda Russell led the way.

Before 1900 (and for some time afterwards), African American cooks like Malinda Russell enabled a particular subset of America's middle class to perform a desirable lifestyle. As the "black back regions" powering white households, that is as the unacknowledged laborers enabling a comfortable and enviable status,[2] cooks, bakers, and their supporting colleagues remained invisible. Like the fictional Downton Abbey servants of British television fame, workers responsible for the running of a smooth household ideally were never seen; enslaved or not, their efforts went unremarked yet were essential. A second-generation freewoman, Russell was shaped by the "peculiar institution" of slavery; generations of cooks, bakers, and confectioners had produced meals and feasts under its daunting conditions. As an ambitious Black person in the post-slavery era, Russell had almost no career paths and few options for entreprencurship, yet paradoxically, the legacy of enslavement illuminated various pathways to economic self-sufficiency. By publishing a collection of recipes, Russell could advertise her culinary expertise, as well as proclaim her literacy and self-reliance. She would do so by relying on two forms already familiar to the American reader, the slave narrative and the hospitality manual, or cook book.

Russell's *Cook Book* first nods, in its introduction, to that genre inextricably associated with African Americans—the slave narrative. This mode of autobiography, describing the birth, trials, and eventual freedom of the narrator, has been called a uniquely American production. Russell, free-born, could not claim a past condition of servitude. "My mother being born after the emancipation of my grandmother, her children are by law free" (3). But by placing her own life next to the experiences of her formerly enslaved relatives and peers, Russell gestures back to the skills enforced by years of unpaid labor and promotes her own expertise. At the time she published her volume, the Black cook in a white household was already a cultural staple. Even if in real life such female household chefs were not deployed in every antebellum home, Harriet Beecher Stowe's best-selling *Uncle Tom's Cabin* (1852), promoted that supposedly ubiquitous presence in the nation's consciousness.[3] Subtly invoking popular notions of the "naturally gifted" African American woman cook through pointing to her own heritage, "A Short History of the Author" asserts that she was "compelled to leave the South on account of of my Union principles, in the time of the Rebellion, and having been robbed of all my hard-earned wages . . . I have put out this book with the intention of benefiting the public as well as myself" (5). Russell sought to fulfill the demand for household manuals and, in so doing, make a better life for herself and her child. Generations of enforced kitchen wisdom assured the cachet of *The Cook Book.*

A second, key, model Russell looked to was already a classic: "I cook after the plan of *The Virginia Housewife*" (5). Telling her readers that she followed in the footsteps of Mary Randolph, a member of the white Virginia elite, promised further proofs of Russell's prowess: Randolph's volume, first published in 1824, went through dozens of printings in the 19th century, and is consulted to this day by Southern chefs bent on resurrecting and refining the highlights of the region's cuisine. Randolph displayed a command of Virginia and European cuisines; Russell would also include standard and southern delicacies. "Sweet Potato Baked Pudding" and "Sweet

Potato Slice Pie" (22–23), were treats more likely to appear in cookbooks appearing south of the Mason-Dixon line. "How to Cook and Dress Ocher"—the vegetable okra, not the pigment (36)—points to African diasporic cuisine. "Christmas Plum Pudding" (22) and "Summer Mince Pie" (25) nod to European favorites. Russell acknowledges her apprenticeship, as well, under "colored" Virginia cook Fanny Steward, bringing together culinary influences from the well-off to the working woman. Whether Russell's recipes were culled from an earlier printed text, concocted by her, or orally transmitted by Steward, we may never know.

LOVE THE HISTORY, you dear reader might say, but what can one do in the 21st century, when faced with a typical recipe from the 19th, much less one by Malinda Russell? Let me walk you into the hidden history of a culinary scholar: In the wake of the publication of my study, *Recipes for Respect*, I appeared in a short feature about Black food history.[4] Part of that mini-documentary took place in my kitchen, where

I ventured to recreate Russell's "cheap gingerbread." In the video, standing in front of a counter that held a rather sorry looking pan of gingerbread, I lamented that her recipe included no useful instructions for those of us who came up in modern kitchens: there's no oven temperature noted, no cake pan size listed, no sequence of steps in which one prepares the batter. "Ginger cake" calls for

> one pint of molasses, one cup butter, one pint milk, one tablespoon ginger, three eggs; add flour to a proper thickness to bake in pans. (p. 11 in original)

Upon deciding I would try Russell's instructions out, I next looked at my go-to gingerbread recipe from Laurie Colwin's *Home Cooking*; there I got a sense of the order in which to prepare and assemble the ingredients, including what type of pan and at what temperature and for how long I should bake the cake.[5] The result? A cake that crested impressively in the oven, only to collapse and crack cavernously as it cooled, greatly resembling a fallen-in volcano cone, if on a smaller scale. One of the best things about reading old cookbooks such as Russell's stems from learning your way around a kitchen in a way entirely new to us working in the age of electric pressure cookers, air fryers, convection ovens, immersion blenders, and the like. To bridge the gap between us in the 21st century, and our American forebears in the kitchens of the 19th century, may be as simple as trying the Sponge Cake recipe from Russell. Consisting solely of an ingredient list—"one lb sugar, half lb flour, ten eggs, juice and grated rind of a lemon"—our experienced cook offers nary a suggestion regarding pan size, oven heat, nor a sense of the batter's consistency. Then, as now, Russell reminds us that cooking, and living, may need less in the way of operating instructions than prior experience—or a cook's ability to depend on serendipity and go with the flow.

RUSSELL TEACHES US MORE than how to bake a cake. Beyond knowing cookery, and much like her male African American predecessors in hotel and housekeeping, Malinda Russell understood the relationship between black cook and white consumer.

She wielded her family members' past servitude paradoxically to substantiate her own expertise as an independent agent. By connecting the Black American past of involuntary work to a culinary compendium, Russell scripted an affirmation of her own talents, even as her gifts referenced a troubling past. Some may have been born enslaved, but their daughters and sons would be known as chefs.

(2024)

Bibliography

Bivins, S. Thomas. *The Southern Cookbook. A Manual of Cooking and List of Menus, Including Recipes Used by Noted Colored Cooks and Prominent Caterers.* Hampton, VA: Press of the Hampton Institute, 1912.

Campbell, Tunis G. *Hotel Keepers, Head Waiters, and House-keepers' Guide.* Boston: Coolidge and Wiley, 1848.

Colwin, Laurie. *Home Cooking.* New York: Knopf, 1988.

Estes, Rufus L. *Good Things to Eat, as suggested by Rufus.* Chicago, 1911.

Fisher, Abby. *What Mrs. Fisher Knows About Old Southern Cooking.* San Francisco: Women's Co-operative Printing Office, 1881.

Foreman, P. Gabrielle. "Manifest in Signs: The Politics of Sex and Representation in *Incidents in the Life of a Slave Girl.*" In Harriet Jacobs and *Incidents in the Life of a Slave Girl: New Critical Essays*, edited by D. Garfield and R. Zafar, 78. Cambridge University Press, 1996.

Glover, E. T. *The Warm Springs receipt-book: compiled between the years 1881 and 1894.* Richmond, VA: B. F. Johnson, 1897.

Hall, H. Franklyn. *How to Make and Serve 100 Choice Broths and Soups.* Philadelphia, 1903.

Hall, H. Franklyn. *300 Ways to Cook and Serve Shell Fish.* Philadelphia, Christian Banner Print, 1901.

Randolph, Mary. *Virginia House-Wife. Method is the soul of management.* Davis and Forth, Washington, DC: 1824.

Roberts, Robert. *The House Servant's Directory. A Monitor for Private Families* Boston: Munroe & Francis, 1828.

Russell, Malinda. *A Domestic Cook Book: Containing a Careful Selection of Useful Receipts for the Kitchen.* Paw Paw, MI, 1866

Stowe, Harriet Beecher. *Uncle Tom's Cabin: or, Life Among the Lowly.* Boston: John P. Jewett, 1852.

Turner, Bertha. *The Federation Cook Book. A Collection of Tested Recipes, contributed by the Colored Women of the State of California.* Pasadena, CA, 1910.

Witt, Doris, and David Lupton. "Chronological Bibliography of Cookbooks by African Americans." In Witt, *Black Hunger: Food and the Politics of U.S. Identity.* New York and Oxford: Oxford University Press, 1999.

Zafar, Rafia. *Recipes for Respect. African American Meals and Meaning.* Athens: University of Georgia Press, 2019.

Notes

1. There are few cookery books by African Americans published before 1914. They include *The Warm Springs Receipt-Book* by E. T. Glover (1897), H. Franklyn Hall's *How to Make and Serve 100 Choice Broths and Soups* (1903) and *300 Ways to Cook and Serve Shell Fish* (1901), Bertha Turner's *The Federation Cookbook* (1910), and S. Thomas Bivins's *The Southern Cookbook* (1912). See Witt and Lupton's bibliography in Witt, 221–28. The Witt & Lupton bibliography does not list Hall's 1903 volume nor his *The Standard American Culinary Encyclopedia*, which is listed as a previous publication on the title page of his *How to Make and Serve 100 Choice Broths and Soups* (1). Early works continue to be identified, as was the case with Malinda Russell's cookbook, re-discovered by culinary historian and bibliophile Janice B. Longone about a year after the Lupton-Witt bibliography appeared. See http://www.nytimes.com/2007/11/21/dining/21cook.html?pagewanted=all Accessed April 8, 2015.

2. P. Gabrielle Foreman, "Manifest in Signs: The Politics of Sex and Representation in *Incidents in the Life of a Slave Girl*," in Harriet Jacobs and *Incidents in the Life of a Slave Girl: New Critical Essays*, eds. D. Garfield and R. Zafar (Cambridge University Press, 1996), 78.

3. Acknowledged to be the best-seller in the nineteenth century United States, after the Bible, *Uncle Tom's Cabin*

included among its main characters Chloe, a plump, preternaturally talented plantation head cook, wife to the eponymous Uncle Tom.

4. To my delight, HEC Media's short was nominated for a Mid-America Emmy. https://hecmedia.org/posts/recipes-for-respect-african-american-meals-and-meanings

5. Readers interested in my tweak of Colwin's recipe may find it in the St. Louis Post-Dispatch, although acknowledgement to the Colwin recipe is not noted (it may have been in the original article, no longer on the website): https://www.stltoday.com/life-entertainment/local/food-drink/cooking/recipes/gingerbread/article_0098beab-785b-5911-b6e0-6b96dce38552.html. If I recall I also noted that yogurt mixed with milk, as per Colwin, or plain kefir can be substituted for the buttermilk.

A DOMESTIC
—————————
COOK BOOK

A Short History of the Author

I was born in Washington County, and raised in Green County, in the eastern part of Tennessee. My mother, Malinda Russell, was a member of one of the first families set free by Mr. Noddie, of Virginia. I am the daughter of Karon, the youngest child of my grandmother. My mother being born after the emancipation of my grandmother, her children are by law free. My mother died when I was quite young. At the age of about nineteen, I set out for Liberia; but being robbed by some member of the party with whom I was traveling, I was obliged to stop at Lynchburgh,

Virginia, where I commenced cooking, and at times traveling with ladies as nurse; and always received the praise of being faithful. The following is a certificate given me by Doct. More at the time I started for Liberia:

> "We, the undersigned, have been acquainted with Malinda Russell, a free woman of color, for the last eight or ten years, and certify that she is a girl of fine disposition and business-doing habits Her moral deportment, of late, has been respectable; and we have little doubt, should she reach Liberia, in Africa, to which place she is now bound, that she will make a valuable citizen."

About this time I married in Virginia. Anderson Vaughan, my husband, lived only four years. I have always been called by my maiden name since his death. I am still a widow, with one child, a son, who is crippled; he has the use of but one hand. While in Virginia, I kept a wash-house. The following is my advertisement:

> "Malinda Vaughan, Fashionable Laundress, would respectfully inform the ladies and Gentlemen of Abingdon, that she is prepared to wash and iron every

description of clothing in the neatest and most satisfactory manner. Every article washed by her, she guarantees shall pass unscathed through the severest ordeal of inspection, without the remotest danger of condemnation. She can conscientiously boast of a proficiency in her business, and all clothing committed to her charge shall be neatly executed and well taken care of. She hopes to receive, as she shall exert herself to deserve, a sufficiency of patronage to insure her a permanent location. Her charges shall correspond with the times. —ABINGDON, MAY 3."

I returned to Tennessee, and, after the death of my husband, kept a boarding-house on Chuckey Mountain, Cold Springs, for three years. My boarders and visitors were from almost every State in the Union, who came to the Springs for their health. After leaving the boarding-house, I kept a pastry shop for about six years, and, by hard labor and economy, saved a considerable sum of money for the support of myself and son, which was taken from me on the 16th of January, 1864, by a guerrilla party, who threatened my life if I revealed who they were. Under those circumstances we were obliged to leave home, following a flag of truce out of the Southern borders, being attacked several times by the enemy.

Hearing that Michigan was the Garden of the West, I resolved to make that my home, at least for the present, until peace is restored, when I think of returning to Greenville, Tennessee, to try and recover at least a part of my property.

This is one reason why I publish my Cook Book, hoping to receive enough from the sale of it to enable me to return home. I know my book will sell well where I have cooked, and am sure those using my receipts will be well satisfied.

Paw Paw, Mich., May, 1866.

Rules And Regulations of the Kitchen
The Kitchen should always be Neat and Clean.
The Tables Pastry Boards, Pans, and everything pertaining to Cookery, should be well Cleansed.

I have made Cooking my employment for the last twenty years, in the first families of Tennessee, (my native place,) Virginia, North Carolina, and Kentucky. I know my Receipts to be good, as they always have given satisfaction. I have been advised to have my Receipts published, as they are valuable, and every family has use for them. Being compelled to leave the South on account of my Union principles, in the time of the Rebellion, and having been robbed of all my hard-earned wages which I had saved; and as I am now advanced in years, with no other means of support than my own labor; I have put out this book with the intention of benefiting the public as well as myself.

I learned my trade of FANNY STEWARD, a colored cook, of Virginia, and have since learned many new things in the art of Cooking.

I cook after the plan of the "Virginia Housewife."

MALINDA RUSSELL.

RECEIPTS

SALT RISING BREAD

To a half pint warm water, a pinch of salt; stir to a thick batter and keep warm until it rises. To one pint of this rising add three pints warm water, a little salt, and a small piece of lard. Knead the dough until smooth, make into rolls, keep warm until it rises; bake quick, but do not scorch.

SOFT GINGER BREAD

Two quarts flour, 3-4ths lb lard, 3-4ths lb sugar, three teaspoonfuls cinnamon, two of ginger, one of allspice, one pint sour milk, molasses to make a stiff batter, one teaspoonful soda dissolved in milk.

SOFT GINGER BREAD

One quart molasses, one cup sugar, 1-4th lb lard, three eggs; beat sugar and eggs well together; one gill sour milk, one tablespoonful soda dissolved in warm water, two table-spoonfuls ginger, flour enough to make a soft dough. Knead well, roll, and bake in a quick oven.

CREAM CAKE

One and a half cup sugar, two cups sour cream, two cups flour, one or two eggs, one teaspoon soda; flavor with lemon.

SALLY DOUGH CAKE

Three cups sugar, one cup yeast, three cups sweet milk, three eggs; beat to a thin batter, set over night. When light, add one cup butter, flour to make a stiff batter. Keep warm until it rises the second time. Paper and grease the pan before rising the last time; bake in a slow oven.

WHITE MOUNTAIN CAKE

One cup white sugar, two eggs, one-half cup butter, one-half cup sweet milk, one-half teaspoonful soda, one teaspoonful cream tartar, two and one-half cups flour.

QUEEN'S PARTY CAKE

One quart sour cream, six lbs sugar, six lbs butter, five lbs raisins, five lbs currants, one and one-half lbs figs, one ounce cloves, one ounce cinnamon, one and one-half nutmeg, extract of lemon or vanilla, whites of eighteen eggs, yelks of ten eggs, one teaspoonful soda, two teaspoonfuls cream tartar, flour to stir quite stiff.

PLAIN POUND CAKE

One lb sugar, one lb flour, one nutmeg, 3-4ths lb butter, twelve eggs, half gill brandy. Paper and grease your pans well; bake in a moderate oven.

CORK CAKE

Three cups sugar, one cup butter, one cup sour cream, five cups flour, five eggs, one teaspoon soda, one teaspoon cream tartar; flavor with lemon.

SPONGE CAKE

One lb sugar, twelve eggs; take out one yelk; ten ounces flour; beat the yelks and sugar together well; beat the whites to a stiff froth; gradually mix together; flavor with lemon; bake with a gradual heat.

DOVER CAKE

Two cups sugar, four eggs, one cup butter, one cup sour cream, three cups unsifted flour, one teaspoon cream tartar, one teaspoon soda; flavor to taste.

WASHINGTON CAKE

Three cups sugar, six eggs, one cup butter, one cup sour milk, one teaspoon soda, three cups flour, one teaspoon cream tartar; flavor with lemon to your taste.

BREAD DOUGH CAKE

One pint light bread dough, three eggs, two cups sugar, one cup butter, fill with fruit or carraway seeds; stir together well, put in cake pan, let it rise, bake moderately. This cake, if made with fruit and iced, will keep a long time.

GRATED BREAD CAKE

Grate one quart stale bread, six eggs, one and a half cup butter, three cups sugar, one pint milk, two teaspoons cream tartar, one teaspoon soda, one grated nutmeg, three tablespoons flour; bake in a moderate oven.

CREAM CAKE

One cup and a half sugar, two cups sour cream, one tea-spoon soda, three cups flour, lightly measured, one grated nutmeg; bake in a moderate oven.

FRUIT CAKE

One lb flour, one lb sugar, 3-4ths lb butter, two lbs seeded raisins, two lbs currants, one lb citron, one and a half lb almonds, half ounce mace, one gill rose water, one wine-glass brandy, ten eggs.

WEDDING CAKE

Three lbs flour, three lbs butter, three lbs sugar, six lbs cur-rants, six lbs raisins, one ounce nutmeg, one ounce cinna-mon, one ounce cloves, half gill brandy, one gill rose water, thirty eggs.

RICH BLACK CAKE

Two cups sugar, one and a half cup molasses, two cups but-ter, one cup sour cream, four cups unsifted flour, eight eggs, one and a half lb raisins, one lb citron, one lb currants, one tablespoon mace, one do. cloves, one do. cinnamon, one wine-glass brandy, one do. rose water, extract of lemon.

MALINDA RUSSELL

FRUIT CAKE

Four eggs, one cup sugar, two cups molasses, one and a half cup butter, one cup new milk, one lb raisins, two cups currants, one teaspoon soda, three ounces cinnamon, nutmeg, citron, four cups flour.

COCOANUT SPONGE CAKE

Quarter lb white sugar, whites of four eggs, beat the eggs to a froth, one tablespoon flour, one grated cocoanut; mix the ingredients, bake in small shape, in a slow oven.

ALLSPICE CAKE

Three-fourths lb butter, one lb flour, eight eggs, half teacup sour cream; beat the yelks, sugar and cream together; one tablespoon cloves, one do. cinnamon, one do. mace, one do. allspice, one gill brandy, lemon extract, one gill rose water, one nutmeg, one small teaspoon soda, one do. cream tartar, mixed in the flour; bake in a moderate oven.

MARBLE CAKE

The White.—Half lb butter, whites of fourteen eggs, 3-4ths lb flour, half gill brandy; flavor with lemon.

The Dark.—The yelks of eight eggs, two teacups sugar, one do. butter, one do. sour cream, four cups flour, half cup molasses, flavor with cinnamon, cloves, nutmeg, or mace; two teaspoons cream tartar, one do. soda; beat the yelks and sugar together until very light. Paper and butter the pan, first a layer of the white, then of the dark, alternately, finishing with the white.

ELIZABETH LEMON CAKE

Two cups sugar, one cup butter, one cup milk, five cups flour, six eggs, one tablespoon cream tartar, rind and juice of one lemon.

ELIZABETH CAKE

Three coffee cups flour, one and a half do. sugar, 3-4ths do. milk, one tablespoon butter, three and a half nutmegs, juice and rind of one lemon, 1-4th lb currants, one tablespoon cream tartar and soda.

CREAM CAKE

Six cups sugar, six do. sour cream, twelve eggs, three cups butter, two teaspoons cream tartar, two do. soda, twelve cups flour; grate two nutmegs to flavor.

MALINDA RUSSELL

STIR CAKE

One cup butter, one do. sugar, two do. flour, one do. milk, two eggs, two even teaspoons cream tartar, one do. soda; flavor.

ALMOND SPONGE CAKE

Three-fourths lb sugar, half lb flour, ten eggs; beat the sugar and yelks together until light; beat the whites to a stiff froth; one and a half lb chopped almonds rubbed in flour stirred in; add the whites of eggs, one gill brandy, half gill rose water, extract lemon.

BRIDE'S CAKE

One lb sugar, one lb butter, whites of twenty-four eggs beaten to a stiff froth, one lb flour; cream the butter, then cream butter and sugar together; mix gradually; one gill brandy; flavor with peach or lemon; bake with gradual heat.

GOLD CAKE

One lb white sugar, one lb flour, 3-4ths lb butter, yelks of twenty eggs; beat sugar and eggs until light; beat half the yelks with the sugar until very light, the rest with the butter; mix together gradually one gill brandy and half gill rose water; mix in the flour one teaspoon cream tartar, half do. soda; bake in a slow oven.

RAISIN CAKE

One lb sugar, one lb sugar, 3-4ths lb butter, twelve eggs, two lbs raisins chopped; beat the sugar and butter together, add the yelks well beaten with butter and sugar, mix with the flour one teaspoon soda and cream tartar, add the whites beaten to a stiff froth, one grated nutmeg, and one gill brandy; bake by a gradual heat.

CITRON CAKE

One lb sugar, 3-4ths pound butter, one lb flour, whites of twenty eggs, one lb citron, sliced thin and rubbed in flour; beat butter and sugar until light; one teaspoon cream tartar and half teaspoon soda mixed in the flour, one gill brandy, one do. rose water; flavor with peach or vanilla.

ROSE CAKE

Three-fourths lb sugar, half lb butter, 3-4ths lb flour, whites of fifteen eggs beaten to a froth; cream the sugar and butter together; add the flour and whites of eggs, half gill brandy, flavor with lemon; one tablespoon cochineal with a small piece of alum tied in a bag soaked in warm water one hour. Grease paper your pan, spread a layer of dough, dip your bag in a solution of warm soda water, then squeeze the bag over the dough; add another laying of dough and cochineal alternately; bake with moderate heat.

LOAF JELL CAKE

One lb sugar, 3-4ths lb butter, one lb flour, ten eggs beaten separately, one gill sour cream or milk, one teaspoon cream tartar, one do. soda, one nutmeg; mix and bake in a loaf until well done. Slice the cake while warm, and spread with jell, laying the slices together and iceing the loaf.

GINGER POUND CAKE

One pint molasses, half lb sugar, half pint sour milk, one teaspoon cream tartar, two do. soda, 1-4th lb lard; melt the butter and lard with the molasses until lukewarm, stirring all the time; five cups flour; beat the sugar and yelks together until light; one tablespoon ginger; add the whites, beaten to a stiff froth; ice while warm.

SPONGE CAKE

One lb sugar, half lb flour, ten eggs, juice and grated rind of a lemon.

SEED CAKES

Four cups flour, one and a half do. cream or milk, one half cup butter, three eggs, one half cup carraway seeds, one teaspoon saleratus, one do. rose water; make into a stiff paste; cut out with a tumbler; bake thirty minutes.

ALMOND SPONGE CAKE

Eight ounces almonds blanched and pounded, two ounces flour, half pound sugar, the yelks of seven eggs, and the whites of five eggs.

QUEEN CHARLOTTE'S CAKE

One lb flour, one lb currants, one lb sugar, half lb butter, four eggs, one gill brandy, one gill wine, one gill cream, spice to taste; bake in a loaf.

MALINDA RUSSELL

LOAF CAKE

Two lbs dried and sifted flour, one pint new milk, blood warm, 1-4th lb butter, 3-4ths lb sugar, one pint home-brewed yeast, three eggs, one lb stoned raisins, one nutmeg, a glass of wine if you like. Rub the butter and sugar to a cream, add the flour and the other ingredients; let it rise over night; bake one hour and a half in a slow oven.

LEMON CAKE

One cup butter, three do. powdered sugar, rubbed to a cream, yelks of five eggs well beaten, one teaspoon soda in a cup of milk, juice and rind of one lemon; add whites of eggs beaten to a stiff froth; sift in four cups flour, and bake.

JELLY CAKE

One half cup butter, two cups sugar, one cup milk, two eggs, two teaspoons cream tartar, one do. soda; mix a little stiff, bake thin; when cold, spread with jelly.

FLANNEL CAKE

One quart sweet milk, stir to a thick batter with flour, two tablespoons yeast; let it rise over night; in the morning break in three eggs, stir in two tablespoons lard.

MUSH CAKE

Make a thin mush; add two tablespoons melted lard, one pint sweet milk, three eggs; mix a batter to the consistency of pancakes. Pour the hot mush into the batter, stirring it well; and bake on a griddle.

COFFEE CAKES

Bake soft boiled rice; add twice as much flour as rice, a handful Indian meal, and a little yeast; mix over night, and bake in the morning.

INDIAN CAKE

Two cups meal, one do. flour, one do. cream, one do. milk, one do. sugar, three eggs, one teaspoon soda, one do. salt.

FRIED RICE CAKES

Rub into a quart bowl of soft boiled rice one cup milk and two eggs; mix till smooth; put out in small cakes with flour enough to form them, and fry.

INDIAN MEAL BATTER CAKES

To one quart Indian meal add one tablespoon lard, and enough hot water to scald the meal; stir it smooth; add enough sour milk to make a batter; break in two eggs; put into a pint of flour two teaspoons of soda and two do. of cream tartar; stir this in last, and bake on a griddle.

RICE BATTER CAKES

One pint, rice; after being cooked, stir in the rice while hot, half pint Indian meal, three eggs, one pint sour milk, one pint flour; melt a tablespoon of butter or lard, stir in the butter, add more milk if too thick, one and a half teaspoon soda; bake on a griddle.

DROP GINGER CAKE

One pint molasses, one cup sugar, one do. sour cream, three eggs, one cup melted butter, three teaspoons soda, one do. cream tartar; heat the molasses and butter together; beat the sugar and eggs together; put the soda and cream tartar in the flour, make a stiff batter, almost a dough; one tablespoon ginger; drop into a buttered dripping-pan; bake moderately, without scorching.

BOILED ICEING

Beat the whites of four eggs to a stiff froth; boil one lb crushed sugar until it ropes and spins off in threads; then turn the boiling sugar slowly over the eggs, stirring thoroughly and beating; flavor with lemon, peach, or vanilla.

SUGAR DROP CAKE

One lb sugar, six eggs, one cup butter, one do. sour cream, half lb stoned raisins, half lb citron, two teaspoons cream tartar, one do. soda; chop raisins and citron fine; half lb English currants, one lb flour; rub the fruit in four ounces more flour, beat the eggs separately, stir the fruit in last; two teaspoons cloves, two do. cinnamon, one grated nutmeg, two teaspoons mace. Butter sheets of paper, lay in a dripping-pan, and bake moderately, iceing while warm.

STRAWBERRY SHORT CAKE

Make the cake the same as cream biscuit; crush and strain the berries, stirring them thick with white sugar, bake in sheets; split the cake while hot, butter well and cover with berries, stack in a steak dish, turn sweet cream over it, and eat while hot for tea.

COLD ICEING

One lb pulverized sugar, break in the whites of five eggs on the sugar, beating with a silver spoon or wooden paddle; pound a lemon and squeeze in the juice.

MALINDA RUSSELL

RASPBERRY TEA CAKE

One cup white sugar, one pint sour cream, three table-spoons melted butter, three cups flour, one and a half tea-spoon soda, two do. cream tartar, grated nutmeg, mix into a batter; pour over sheet paper into dripping-pan; bake in a quick oven; when done, cut into squares, crush the berries, and sweeten to your taste. Cover the cake with berries, and stack the same as Gell Cake.

WAFER CAKE

Three-fourths lb sugar, 1-4th lb butter, eight eggs, half lb flour; cream the butter; beat the yelks, butter, and sugar together until light, beat the whites to a stiff froth, add all together, stir to a batter, drop into greased wafer irons, bake in a minute, take while hot, roll them up and ice them.

OLD MAIDS

Whites of three eggs beaten to a stiff froth, one cup white sugar, half cup flour, flavor with lemon, stir to a batter, and fry in hot lard. When done, grate white sugar over them.

BOILED ICEING

One lb white coffee sugar, boiled until it ropes; beat the whites of three eggs to a stiff froth; turn the hot sugar slowly over the egg, beating until it cools, then flavor with extract of lemon.

SHORT CAKE

One half lb butter, one pint sweet milk, soda the size of a bean; mould quickly, not very stiff, roll into sheets, bake in a brisk oven.

FRIED CAKES

Two and a half cups sugar, one cup sour milk, three eggs, one cup butter, one teaspoon soda; roll; cut with fried cake cutter.

LEMON CAKE

Cream one lb butter and one of sugar together; beat the yelks of twelve eggs and add to the butter and sugar; beat the whites to a stiff froth, add one lb flour and the whites gradually, one teaspoon soda and cream tartar, in the flour grate the rind and juice of a lemon; bake in moderately; flavor with extract of lemon.

MALINDA RUSSELL

PLUM CAKE

One lb sugar, one do. butter, eight eggs, one lb flour, three lbs stoned raisins, three do. currants and citron, one glass wine, one do. brandy, one half teacup molasses; spice to taste.

PLUM CAKE

Three lbs flour, three do. raisins, three do. butter, three do. sugar, thirty eggs, four lbs currants, half ounce cloves, one nutmeg, half lb citron, one tablespoon ginger.

SOFT GINGER CAKE

One lb flour, one do. butter, nine eggs, two quarts milk, a little yeast; mix together warm.

SOFT GINGER CAKE

One cup butter, one do. sour milk, three do. molasses, five do. flour, three eggs, two teaspoons soda, raisins or currants.

GINGER CAKE

One pint molasses, one cup butter, one pint milk, one tablespoon ginger, three eggs; add flour to make a proper thickness to bake in pans.

SPONGE CAKE

Eight eggs, one lb sugar, half lb flour, a little salt.

POUND CAKE

One lb sugar, one do. flour, 3-4ths do. butter, eight eggs.

SWEET TEA CAKE

One quart milk, one coffee cup butter, one lb sugar, yeast to raise.

NAMELESS CAKE

One teacup butter, one do. sugar, five eggs, one cup milk, two cups flour.

SODA CAKE

Three teacups sugar, one do. butter, five do. flour, the whites of seven eggs, two teaspoons cream tartar, a scant one of soda, one cup sweet milk, the grated rind of a lemon; add the cream tartar to the flour, soda to the milk.

DROP CAKE

One pint flour, half lb butter, half lb sugar, half of a nutmeg, a handful of currants, two eggs, a large pinch of soda; bake ten or fifteen minutes.

MALINDA RUSSELL

CHEAP SPONGE CAKE

One cup flour, two eggs, one cup sugar, large spoon sweet milk, half spoon soda, one spoon cream tartar, a little salt, grated rind of one lemon, one teaspoon butter; bake fifteen minutes.

SPONGE CAKE

Two cups sugar, two do. flour, six eggs, two teaspoons of cream tartar. Put in the flour one teaspoon soda dissolved in a little milk, and stirred in when going into the oven.

NEW YEAR'S CAKE

Three and a half lbs. flour, 3-4ths lb butter, 1-4th lb powdered sugar, seven eggs, half ounce ammonia, half pint milk.

SHREWSBERY CAKE

One lb flour, one do. butter, one do. sugar, the whites of sixteen eggs, spice to your taste.

ICEING

One lb sugar, whites of three eggs, cold water enough to wet the sugar. Beat the eggs a little, put them in the sugar; let it boil until it thickens, stirring it thoroughly all the time.

FRENCH LADY CAKE

Three cups sugar, one do. butter, six eggs, one cup sweet milk, one teaspoon soda, two do. cream tartar, one wine-glass brandy, the juice of one lemon, four cups flour; the soda dissolved in the milk, the cream tartar in the flour.

GRAHAM CAKES

One quart buttermilk, three eggs, one pint cooked rice, a little salt, one tablespoon cream tartar, half tablespoon soda, flour to make a thin batter; bake on a griddle.

[Remarks.—As a great many ladies have wished to know how I have such good success in making my cakes so light, I will say, I first heat the oven hot enough for cooking, set in my cake, and open the door; and for a common sized cake leave the door open for about fifteen minutes, and for a large one, about twenty minutes. When the cake begins to raise, close the door.]

MRS. ROE'S CREAM PIE

One cup good sweet cream, the whites of three eggs beaten to a froth, one cup coffee sugar, the juice of one lemon. Bake with a rich under crust.

CONELL RISING

Take half a teacupful of conell with a little salt, turn boiling water over it, stir it quite thin, keep it warm; set it one morning to bake the next. The bread made the same as salt rising bread, using two or three table spoonfuls of the yeast.

MUFFINS

Seven eggs well beaten, one quart sweet milk, three tablespoons melted lard, a lump of soda the size of a bean, flour to make a thin batter. Butter the muffin ring, and bake in a quick oven.

GINGER SPONGE

Two cups molasses, one do. sugar, one do. butter, five eggs, two cups sour milk, two teaspoons soda, two do. cream tartar, two do. ginger, one do. cloves, one do. cinnamon, five cups flour.

CINNAMON COOKIES

One cup sweet cream, two do. sugar, three eggs, half cup butter, two tablespoons ground cinnamon. Beat the eggs and sugar well; melt the butter; stir it with the eggs and sugar till smooth; then add the cream, one teaspoon cream tartar, half teaspoon soda, flour to make a soft dough; roll thin, and bake in a quick oven.

GINGER CRACKERS

One pint molasses, one pint sugar, one teacup lard, one cup butter, one teaspoon soda; melt the molasses, lard and butter together, until lukewarm; the yelks of eight eggs; beat the eggs and sugar together till light; one tablespoon ginger, one do. cinnamon, one do. cloves, one do. lemon, one nutmeg. Add the ingredients together, with flour enough to make a stiff dough; knead well, roll thin, and bake in a quick oven; cut with cake cutters.

COOKIES

One lb white sugar, one pint cream, one ounce ammonia; flour to roll.

COOKIES

One cup sugar, one do. sour cream, one do. butter, one teaspoon soda; flour to roll out.

MALINDA RUSSELL

COOKIES

Three teacups sugar, four eggs, one cup butter, one do.
sour milk, half teaspoon soda; flavor to taste; soft dough;
roll thin, and bake in a quick oven.

JUMBLES

One lb sugar, half lb butter, seven eggs, one nutmeg, one
teaspoon cream tartar, half teaspoon soda, flour to make
a soft dough, half teacup sweet cream; cream the butter;
beat the sugar and eggs together until quite light; roll and
cut them; bake in a moderate oven.

JUMBLES

One lb flour, 3-4ths lb sugar, one half lb butter, five eggs,
mace, rose water, and carraway, to your taste.

GINGER SNAPS

One cup molasses, half cup sugar, half cup butter, half cup
boiling water, teaspoon soda, two tablespoons ginger; pour
the boiling water over the butter, dissolve the soda in the
water and butter, then stir it to a cream; mix all together,
with flour to make a stiff dough, roll thin, and bake in a
quick oven.

WHITE SUGAR CRACKERS

Half lb sugar, 1-4th lb butter, whites of ten eggs beaten to a stiff froth, half lb raisins seeded and chopped, half tablespoon lemon, one tablespoon rose water. Cream the butter, beat sugar and butter together until light; add the ingredients together, flour to make a soft dough; run it through the jumble moulds, sprinkle it over with white sugar, bake in a moderate oven; ice when cool.

FLOATING ISLAND

One quart rich sweet cream, one lb loaf sugar, one pint Cognac brandy, one gill wine, six eggs broken into the cream; churn in a whip churn to a stiff froth, spread with gell slices of pound cake, and lay it in the bottom of a float dish, and turn the float over it.

BOILED CUSTARD

Beat with six eggs sufficient sugar to sweeten the custard, then boil half gallon new milk; stir in slowly the eggs and sugar, stirring all the time; flavor with cinnamon bark, boiling it in the milk.

MALINDA RUSSELL

WHIP TRIFLE

Two quarts sweet cream, sugar to sweeten, one pint wine, one gill brandy, juice of one lemon, whites of six eggs; flavor with extract of lemon; churn well in a whip churn, cut small pieces of sponge cake, laying it in a float bowl; the trifle to be turned over it after taking off the froth—putting the froth in wine glasses and setting around the float bowl.

WINE GELL

Two packages gelatine, one quart wine, one quart water. Put into a kettle and simmer, pounding and squeezing in the juice of two lemons, break in six eggs, simmer all together 20 or 30 minutes; pour into a flannel bag and let it drip; the first that drips turn back into the bag, letting it drip again. Pour into moulds, and set it away to gell.

GINGER PUDDING

One and a half cups molasses, half cup sugar, three eggs, one cup sour milk, half cup butter, three cups flour lightly measured, one teaspoon soda, one do. ginger, one do. cloves, bake in quick oven.

CHARLOTTE RUSSE

One pint milk, 3-4ths lb sugar, half box gelatine. Put these together, and set over a kettle of boiling water after the gelatine is dissolved; beat four eggs and stir in; leave over the fire until it looks clear, then let it cool. Beat to a stiff froth one pint cream, add vanilla to taste; stir all together well and set in a cool place, with ice or snow around it. When you add the eggs, stir thoroughly; when cool, give it a hard beat. Put cake in a mould stuck together with white of egg, and put the liquid inside, or serve the cake and liquid separately.

APPLE JELL

One peck pared and cored tart apples, two quarts water; boil and strain through a bag without pressing; let it drip over night; one pint sugar to two pints juice; boil quickly to a gell.

BLACKBERRY WINE

To one gallon berries pour over them one quart boiling water, crush the berries and strain through a hair sieve; add three pounds sugar to one gallon juice, turn into a stone pot and let it stand till through singing, skimming every morning; tie over the top a thin cloth, bottle and cork tight when through singing.

BLACKBERRY CORDIAL

Boil a sufficient quantity of berries to make a gallon of juice; boil in a stone pot, setting it in hot water; strain through a bag; add three lbs white sugar to a gallon of juice; when cool, pour in one quart brandy; bottle and cork tight.

STRAWBERRY CORDIAL

Two and a half lbs sugar to one gallon juice; put the berries in a stone pot, setting it in hot water, boil and strain through a bag, mix the sugar with the juice, simmer half an hour; when cold, add a quart of peach brandy, bottle and cork.

QUINCE CORDIAL

Pare and core one half bushel quinces, putting into a brass kettle with two quarts water, cook well, drain through a sieve, and then through a bag, adding two and a half lbs sugar to a gallon juice; boil 15 or twenty minutes. When cold, add one quart brandy to one gallon juice, bottle and cork.

RICE MILK

One pint boiled rice to one gallon milk, twelve eggs; sweeten to your taste, and flavor with lemon.

CHOPPED APPLE PIE

Chop your tart apples, break in six eggs, half lb sugar, half lb butter melted; beat all together, flavor with nutmeg and cinnamon, adding one gill brandy and one gill wine. Paste the plate, laying pastry over the top, and bake.

BAKED INDIAN MEAL PUDDING

Make a thin mush, beat six or eight eggs, stir in the mush half teacup butter, make a batter thick of flour and sweet milk, putting in the eggs. Stir the mush in the batter until smooth, grate in a nutmeg, bake slowly in a pudding pan; eat with rich sauce.

BAKED APPLE PUDDING

Pare and core twelve apples, put them into a pudding dish, with one cup sugar and two of water; put in cloves and cinnamon; set them in a slow oven to bake; beat the yelks of six eggs with one cup sugar, one pint milk, two tablespoons flour, turn this over the apples, and cook until done; beat the whites of six eggs lightly with a little white sugar, flavor with lemon; turn this over the fruit just before taking from the oven; to be eaten with rich cream.

SPICED CURRANTS

Five lbs ripe currants, five lbs sugar, two tablespoons cinnamon, two do. cloves, one pint vinegar; boil two hours, or more, till quite thick.

CURRANT JELLY WITHOUT COOKING

Equal parts of juice and sugar. Stir it for three hours, and put it in glasses. It will be firm jelly within three days.

CHOW CHOW

One peck green tomatoes, half-a-dozen peppers, one dozen onions, grated horse-radish; chop and scald in salt and water, drain in a sieve, put into jars and pour spiced vinegar over it.

LEMON JELLY

One and a half ounces isinglass, one and a half lbs sugar, four lemons, three pints boiling water. Lay the isinglass in cold water half an hour, take it out and put it with the sugar and lemons sliced. Pour on the boiling water, stirring it all the time; strain through a jelly bag. In warm weather, it will require more isinglass to stiffen well.

TO CLARIFY SUGAR FOR PRESERVING

For each lb of sugar allow half a pint of water; for every three lbs, the white of one egg. Mix when cold, boil a few minutes and skim; let it stand ten minutes, skim again, and strain it.

RIPE TOMATO PICKLES

Prick tomatoes full of holes, let them stand in salt and water two days; then put them into fresh water one day, then scald them in vinegar. Peel and slice one dozen onions; put into a jar a layer of onions, tomatoes, ginger, pepper, mustard and cloves, alternately, until the jar is filled.

MALINDA RUSSELL

TOMATO CATSUP

To one gallon tomatoes add four tablespoons cloves, one do. mace, one do. cayenne, two do. allspice, eight tablespoons of white mustard seed, two whole peppers, one ounce garlic, one pint good vinegar. Boil away nearly half, strain, bottle and cork tight.

RASPBERRY JAM

Allow one lb of sugar to one lb of fruit; boil the fruit half an hour; strain one quarter of the fruit, and throw away the seeds; add the sugar, and boil the whole ten minutes.

GOOSEBERRY JELL

Put your berries into a stone pot, set it in a kettle of boiling water, covering it tight; let it stand until they burst; run through a sieve, and strain through a bag. Allow one lb and a quarter sugar to one pint of juice; boil quick to a jell.

RIPE CHERRY PIE

Remove the stems and stones; cover the bottom of a long tin with the fruit, to which add a teacup of sugar and one of flour; bake with an upper and under crust.

CRANBERRY JAM

One quart raw cranberries to one lb white sugar. Simmer the fruit one hour after adding the sugar, stirring all the time. Put into bottles or jars, corking tight. Ready for any season.

PEACH MARMALADE

Take clingstone peaches, peel and separate from the pits, put them into a preserving bottle, with water enough to cook them done; mash them fine, and stir them until smooth. To every lb of fruit add 3-4ths of a lb white sugar, which is best to make them clear. Stir three hours, cooking slowly. This will keep two or three years by keeping it in sealed jars.

SPICED CURRANTS

Five lbs currants, four lbs sugar, one cup vinegar, tablespoon cloves ground, two tablespoons pulverized cinnamon.

DRIED RIPE MULBERRIES

Stem and scald the fruit. Take one gallon berries to one and a half lbs sugar, drain them from the syrup, lay them on a platter, boil down the syrup quite thick, and turn it over the fruit. Set it in an oven to dry, be careful not to scorch them. To be used the same as raisins for cakes or puddings. Put them into glass jars and seal tight.

GREEN TOMATO PRESERVES

Five lbs green tomatoes sliced, half tablespoon alum pow-dered, one tablespoon salt, one gallon water; let them stand in this water twelve hours; turn this off and put on fresh water, and let it stand two hours. Take five lbs white sugar, and water enough to make the syrup; put in the syrup, let it scald twenty minutes; lift it out on a platter to stand twelve hours. Let the syrup come to a boil, turn in the tomatoes and boil one hour, then skim out the fruit and let the syrup boil. Put the fruit into jars—a layer of fruit sprinkled over with pieces of orange peel, grains of cloves, and pieces of cinnamon, alternately, until the jar is filled. Pour it over the syrup hot, and seal tight.

PEACH CORDIAL

Pare ripe cling peaches enough to make a gallon of juice; boil and strain them; add three lbs sugar, and simmer half an hour; when cool, add one quart peach brandy; bottle and cork.

RIPE CHERRY PIE

Stem and stone the fruit. Paste a large pudding dish, take out the cherries from the juice, fill the dish and cover with paste; set in the oven to bake, boil the juice quite thick, sweeten to your taste. When cold, add one pint sweet cream to the syrup; take off the top crust and turn the syrup over the cherries, returning the crust.

RIPE PLUM PUDDING

One pint sour milk, half lb butter made into a dough, half teaspoon soda; roll into a large sheet half a gallon stoned plums; scald and flour the sack, put the sheet of dough into the sack, turn in the fruit and pinch the dough together at the top, tie the sack tight and boil two hours. For the sauce, half lb butter, and one lb butter; cream butter and sugar together; break in three eggs, beat it until light; make it into rolls, to be sliced and eaten with the pudding.

BOILED BATTER PUDDING

Three pints sweet milk, eight eggs, one teaspoon soda, two do. salt; put into a bag, and boil three hours. Sauce—Rub together butter and sugar, break in three eggs, and stir till light; one grated nutmeg.

CHRISTMAS PLUM PUDDING

One lb seeded raisins, one do. currants, one do. flour, half
do. bread crumbs, half do. suet, ten eggs, 1-4th lb citron,
and one pint milk. It should be boiled at least three hours;
eaten with sauce composed of sugar, butter and brandy,
beaten very light.

COLD WATER BISCUIT

To one pint cold water, a piece of lard the size of a teacup,
one and a half teaspoon salt; work it lightly in the pastry
bowl, turn out on the dough board, and knead and pound
until it blisters. Mould into biscuit, and bake in a hot oven.

TO MAKE LARD PASTRY

Two quarts flour, one and a half lb lard; divide the lard
into four parts; rub one part into the flour with a knife,
mix with cold water to a consistent dough, roll the dough
into sheets, spreading the remainder of the lard over them,
folding the sheets and rolling again; salt-spoon of salt. Nice
and flaky.

PUFF PASTE

One and a half lb flour, 3-4ths do. butter; rub a quarter of the butter, together with two teaspoons cream tartar and half teaspoon soda, into the flour; spread the remainder of the butter over the sheets, fold and roll again thin, and bake in patties for tarts.

RICE PUDDING BOILED

Pick and scald one quart rice; stone two lbs raisins; rub rice and raisins together until thoroughly mixed, put in a bag into boiling water, boil one hour. Make a sauce of one lb butter, one and a half do. sugar, three pints water, one pint brandy, nutmeg and lemon.

WHORTLEBERRY BOILED PUDDING

Eight eggs, one quart sour milk, two tablespoons lard, flour to make a stiff batter, a little salt. Sprinkle them with dry flour, rub them well, mixing them with the batter; scald the bag, and sprinkle it with dry flour; turn it in, leaving room to rise. Boil with or without a ham; eat with cream sauce or wine.

MALINDA RUSSELL

44

SWEET POTATO BAKED PUDDING

Boil six or eight large sweet potatoes, peel them, strain through a colander, separate six eggs and one cup sugar, beat the yelks and sugar together until light, mix the potato and one cup butter while the potato is warm; beat the whites to a stiff froth, and add them last; flavor with nutmeg, a cup sweet cream three tablespoons flour.

SLICE APPLE PIE

Paste a pudding dish; first a layer of sliced apples, sugar to taste, cloves, nutmeg, cinnamon, and ginger, alternately, until filled; add half pint water and one gill wine; cover with rich pastry and bake until done. To be eaten with sauce.

SWEET POTATO SLICE PIE

Made in the same manner as above, adding one gill brandy, one do. vinegar, half pint water, one grated lemon, rind and juice, sugar to taste; paste the dish, cover the top; eat with sauce.

COOKIES

Two cups sugar, two do. sour milk, one cup butter, one teaspoon soda, one do. cream tartar, flour to make soft dough, ground carraway seeds; sprinkle top with white sugar, roll and cut.

APPLE CUSTARD

Boil and strain one quart apples, one half lb sugar, 1-4th lb butter, six eggs, one pint sweet cream, one gill brandy, one gill wine; beat the sugar and yelks together until light, melt the butter, cream the butter and apples together; separate the eggs, beat the whites to a froth, put the whites in last, flavor with lemon; line a dish with paste, and turn in the custard; bake in hot oven.

IRISH POTATO CUSTARD

Boil and strain through a sieve one dozen good sized pota-toes; rub through the sieve with the potato half lb butter, half lb sugar, eight eggs; cream together the sugar, yelks, and potato; stir in one pint sweet cream, one pint brandy, one gill rose water; lemon to the taste, Paste the dish richly made, fill the dish, and bake in a slow oven.

PAP CUSTARD

One quart sweet milk, boiled and thickened very thick with flour, nearly half lb butter; melt the butter in the boiling milk; twelve eggs, the whites beaten to a froth, yelks and sugar one lb, creamed; flavor with nutmeg and lemon; add the whites before flavoring. Paste and bake in plates.

CHEAP GINGER BREAD

One cup sugar, half cup molasses, two tablespoons melted lard, two cups sour milk, two teaspoons ginger, two do. soda. Mix to a soft dough, roll and bake.

CARVIES' PLUM PUDDING

Three eggs, eight Boston Crackers, one pint milk, 1-4th lb melted butter, one and a half cup sugar, one and a half lb stoned and chopped raisins, half teaspoon nutmeg, half teaspoon cloves, half teaspoon cinnamon. Bake or steam three or four hours.

SALLY LUN

Three tablespoons yeast, two do. butter, two do. sugar, two eggs, flour to make thick as cake. Let it rise six hours; bake quick.

FRENCH TEA BISCUIT

Two lbs flour, two ounces butter, half pint sweet milk, one egg, half cup sugar, one cup yeast, half teaspoon soda.

LEMON PUFF

Six eggs, one pint sweet milk, five tablespoons flour, a little salt; bake in cups full twenty minutes. Sauce—Juice of one lemon, put in as much sugar as you can beat the whites of three eggs, pour over the top; eat while hot.

CRULLERS

Two cups sugar, one cup butter, one do. sour milk, six eggs, one teaspoon soda, grated nutmeg, flour to mix a soft dough; boil in lard.

MARY'S JUMBLES

One lb flour, half lb butter, 3-4ths lb sugar, five eggs; any spice you like.

APPLE FLOAT

Boil twelve large apples, remove the skin and strain through a sieve, beat the whites of ten eggs to a stiff froth, sweeten to the taste, and beat with an egg whip one hour, flavor with lemon; to be eaten with cream.

BOILED TRIFLE

One half gallon boiled milk, eight eggs, leaving out the whites of six; beat the remainder with one half lb sugar till light; turn the boiling milk over the eggs, stirring briskly, then turn back into the kettle, stirring all the while; boil six or eight minutes, flavoring with cinnamon or lemon peel. Beat the whites of six eggs to a stiff froth, turning in a glass of gell, beating well; lay in a glass dish three or four slices sponge cake, pour over the cake one half pint brandy. When the trifles cool, pour into the dish, float it with the eggs and gell.

BUTTER PASTRY

One lb eight ounces flour to one lb butter; cream and beat all the water out of the butter; have it firm. Quarter the butter into four quarters, taking out four ounces of the flour; take one quarter of the butter and mix with the large quantity of the flour, stirring with a knife, not using the hand; roll the dough very lightly, sprinkling over the sheets the remaining flour and spreading them over with the butter, folding and rolling alternately. Lay away the dough on the slab, leave it one hour, cut in small pieces, roll thin, lay three sheets in a patty and bake. To be used for tarts.

CREAM CRACKERS

Half pint water, one quart sour cream, half lb butter, half teaspoon soda, flour to mix a stiff dough, knead it well until it blisters, as you do biscuit; to this quantity of dough lay on 3-4ths lb butter, roll thin, spreading the butter over it, sprinkling with flour, folding and rolling again.

TO MAKE HOP ROLLS

One quart warm milk, melt in it a small piece of lard; beat the yelk of one egg in one spoonful of sugar, mix in flour to make a stiff batter, stir in three tablespoons of hop yeast, set away to rise till morning, work in flour to make a soft dough; if sour, add a little soda, make into rolls, rise, and bake in a quick oven.

MINCE PIES

Five lbs beef, four lbs suet, five lbs raisins, five lbs sugar, one lb citron, eight crackers pounded fine, two lemons chopped fine, three pints cider, one quart molasses, one quart wine, one quart brandy, one gill rose water, one quince boiled and chopped, two tablespoons salt, eight teaspoons cloves, thirteen do. cinnamon, four do. mace; grate nutmeg on the top of the pie; add bits of sugar before baking. Mix molasses, crackers, cider and spice, together, heat to almost a scald, then mix it with the remainder of the ingredients. Mix the sugar with the wine. If you like them richer, add fruits, sugar, and spice.

CRACKER PIE

One Boston cracker, one cup water, juice and grated rind of a lemon, one cup sugar, piece of butter the size of a butternut. This makes one pie.

SUMMER MINCE PIE

Four crackers, one and a half cup sugar, one cup molasses, one do. cider, one do. water, two-thirds do. butter, one cup chopped raisins, two eggs well beaten, and stirred in the last thing. Brandy and spice to taste.

MOLASSES CUSTARD

One quart molasses, eight eggs, half lb butter; beat the eggs, then beat eggs and molasses together until light; add ginger, nutmeg, and cinnamon.

LEMON CUSTARD

Yelks of twenty-four eggs, one lb butter, two grated lemons; grate peeling and press out the juice; beat the butter, eggs, and one lb sugar together until very light, flavor with lemon acid, line the dish with paste, and bake.

GREEN CORN BREAD

Three dozen ears of corn grated, one egg, milk, a little salt.

SODA ROLLS

To one gallon flour add one full tablespoon soda, and sufficient sour milk to make a soft dough; knead well, make it into large rolls. Grease your hands well with lard, pat the rolls rough, lay them into pans, and bake in a slow oven.

MALINDA RUSSELL

CREAM TARTAR ROLLS

Three pints flour, a piece of butter half the size of a hen's egg rubbed into the flour; mix through the flour one table-spoon cream tartar, dissolve in sweet milk one teaspoon soda, knead and pound well, make in small rolls, and bake in a quick oven.

INDIAN MEAL BATTER BREAD

One quart Indian meal, half pint flour, three eggs, two tablespoons melted lard, one cup and a half of sour milk, half cup hot water, one teaspoon soda; stir well together, bake in a quick oven.

TOMATO CATSUP

One gallon tomatoes, four tablespoons salt, four do. cloves, one do. Cayenne, two do. allspice, eight do. white mustard seed, two whole peppers, one ounce garlic, one pint good vinegar. Boil away nearly half, strain and bottle; cork tight.

PICKLED STURTIONS

Soak them three days in salt and water, then pour off the brine and pour on scalding hot vinegar.

PICKLED CAULIFLOWER

Cook the cauliflower tender, put it in a jar, pour vinegar and good ground mustard scalded together over them.

PICKLED PEACHES

To one gallon vinegar add four lbs sugar; boil and scum. Take clingstone peaches, fully ripe, rub off the down, stick into each three or four cloves, put into a stone jar, pour over them the boiling liquid, cover the jar closely, set in a cool place for a week or two. Pour off the liquor and boil as before, then return it to the fruit boiling hot; cover carefully for future use.

BRANDY PEACHES

Three dozen large ripe peaches, drop into hot ley, remove them quickly, rub off the fur, drop them into cold water, let them soak while preparing the syrup. Take three lbs sugar to one quart peach brandy, boil to a syrup, drop in the peaches, let them barely scald, lift them out on a platter and let them drip, put them into a glass jar, cook the syrup well; before putting the syrup on, turn over them half a pint of peach brandy, then pour on the syrup, and put up in jars. Use white sugar.

PRESERVED PEACHES

Five lbs sugar to five lbs peaches; while the syrup is making prepare your fruit. Make the syrup of half the sugar, put the peaches in the boiling syrup, cook about ten minutes; dip them out and lay on platters until the next day; drain off the juice from them, putting it with the remainder of the sugar into the kettle and boiling to a thick syrup before adding the fruit, which must cook a few minutes, then lift them out carefully and put in jars; boil the syrup until waxy, then turn over the peaches.

PRESERVED QUINCE

Prepare your syrup; when boiling, pare and core your quinces, drop them in the liquid, and let them remain three or four minutes. Skim them out and lay on platters, then boil the syrup till thick; drain the quinces, then weigh them, allowing one lb sugar to one lb of fruit; put all in the kettle and boil about twenty minutes; put the fruit in jars, and turn over them the syrup.

FRIED RUSK

Two cups sugar, half cup butter, half cup yeast, half pint sweet milk, three eggs, flour to make a thick batter; set

away to rise; when light mix to a dough, rise again; roll;
cut and fry.

MUFFINS

One pint milk, half cup butter, yeast and a little salt, flour
to make a batter.

PICKLED PLUMS

To seven lbs plums take three lbs sugar, one quart vinegar, spice to your taste. Scald every day until the plums
are cooked.

JUMBLES

One cup of sugar, one cup of butter, one egg, a lump of soda
the size of a nutmeg.

CRACKERS

One pint of milk, four ounces of butter, four eggs, flour as
stiff as you can make it.

BURST-UP RICE

Pick and wash a teacup of rice; turn over it boiling water;
turn it off, and turn it into a pint of boiling water; boil hard
in a tin basin closely covered; cook dry; season when done.
Rice cooked in this way is always white and nice.

MALINDA RUSSELL

ONION CUSTARD

Pare and boil twelve large onions; mash when cooked soft, and strain through a sieve; stir in, while hot, 1-4th of a lb of butter; beat half a lb sugar with the yelks of six eggs; stir into the sugar three tablespoons flour, one pint rich cream; stir all together until smooth; one tablespoon cinnamon, half spoon cloves; stir well; beat the whites of the eggs, and stir it in last; paste your pans with rich pastry; bake in a quick oven.

CRANBERRY BAKED PUDDING

Paste your pans with a thick rich crust, and cover it with berries; add a little sugar if you like; then cover with a thin crust, and fill with berries until four layings, then bake in a moderate oven; eat with cream and sugar, or wine sauce.

BAKED BATTER PUDDING

Twelve eggs, half gallon sweet milk; beat the eggs until light; flour to make a good batter; stir in a small teacupful of grains of allspice, a little salt to your taste. Bake in a deep pan or Dutch oven. To be eaten with sweet cream flavored with lemon or vanilla.

RUSK

One lb sugar, seven eggs, half lb butter, one teacup good hop yeast, made into a stiff batter over night; when light, work it into a soft dough in the morning; let it rise again; make it out into rolls; rise again; put a little soda in the flour if sour; bake in a slow oven.

FRIED DOUGHNUTS

One pint sour milk, three eggs, two tablespoons lard, one teaspoon soda, salt, flour to make a not very stiff dough. Roll into sheets, cut, and fry in boiling fat.

BAKERS' GINGER BREAD

One quart molasses, quarter lb lard, three eggs, one gill sour cream, one tablespoon soda, two tablespoons ginger, half tablespoon cloves, one tablespoon cream tartar, flour to make a soft dough; put the soda and cream tartar in the flour, knead well, roll, cut in squares, and bake on sheets.

PRESERVED ORANGES

Boil the oranges till you can run a straw through the skin. Clarify 3-4ths of a lb of sugar for each lb of fruit. Take the oranges from the water, and pour the hot syrup on them. Let them stand one night; next day boil them until the syrup is thick and clear.

QUINCE MARMALADE

Rub the quinces with a cloth, cut in quarters; stew them in a little water till tender enough to rub through a sieve. When strained, put a lb of brown sugar to a lb of flour; set it on the fire, and cook slowly until enough to cut smooth.

ORANGE MARMALADE

Boil the fruit, rub them through a sieve, take one pint of sugar to one of orange; simmer slowly until it is a thick gell. Seal tight in jars.

BLANC MANGE

Three pints sweet milk to half lb Irish moss; boil and stir frequently, sweeten to your taste, and flavor with vanilla or lemon. Strain through a bag, and turn into moulds.

MINUTE PUDDING

One quart milk, two or three eggs, and a little salt. When the milk boils, stir in flour until thick enough to cut with a spoon or knife. Sauce—cream and sugar; flavor with nutmeg, lemon, and vanilla.

GINGER NUTS

One cup sugar, one do. molasses, three eggs, half cup butter, half cup sour cream, one tablespoon ginger, half do. cloves, full teaspoon soda. Beat the sugar and eggs together till light; melt the butter and molasses together; add all together, with flour to make a soft dough; roll, cut, and bake in a quick oven.

SPONGE PUDDING

One lb sugar, twelve eggs, half lb flour, two tablespoons ground cinnamon. Beat the sugar and yelks together until very light, and the whites to a stiff froth; add the flour with the white eggs, stirring very lightly. Sauce—half pint brandy, one pint water, two cups sugar, quarter lb butter; flavor with peach. To be eaten while warm.

MALINDA RUSSELL

BAKED BERRY ROLLS

Rub lard with flour with a little salt, water or milk to make sufficient dough; roll thin; spread over with berries; roll up the crust and put into a dripping-pan in rolls close together until full, then put into the pan butter, sugar and water; bake slowly. Sauce—butter, sugar, brandy and water.

POTATO FERMENT ROLLS

One pint of water, one do. sweet milk, one do. yeast, a little salt, flour enough to make a soft dough. When light, work in lard or butter if sour, work in a little soda with the flour, knead well, then break in a couple of eggs, knead well, make into small rolls, and set where it will keep warm; it will rise in a few minutes; bake in a quick oven.

APPLE JELLY

Slice thirteen large apples very thin without paring them, then cover with water, boil and strain, and to the juice add a half lb white sugar, and as much lemon as your taste may direct. Clarify with egg, and boil to a jelly.

MUTTON CHOP PIE

Stew the mutton and season. Paste the side of the dripping-pan, put in the meat with a strip of the crust rolled thin. Pour over it the gravy, and cover with a crust.

BAKED PEACH COBBLER

Scald and rub the peaches; stew until done; season with sugar to your taste. Paste your pans, put in the fruit, dropping small pieces of butter over it; cover with paste and bake. When done, float the pie with the syrup from the fruit.

COCOANUT PIE

One large cocoanut grated, the milk of the same, and four rolled crackers. Boil two quarts of milk, a small piece of butter, four eggs, the rind of one grated lemon. Sweeten to taste; paste at the bottom.

JUICE LEMON PIE

Two lemons, three eggs, one teaspoon flour, little lump of butter, little salt; grate the rind of the lemon, squeeze out the juice, peel out the pulp; add all together; beat eggs, sugar, and lemon together; add sugar enough to fill a large bowl, and bake twenty minutes. This quantity will make two pies.

MACCARONI

One pound powdered sugar, one pound almonds, the whites of four eggs, two teaspoons extract lemon.

STEAM PLUM PUDDING

One cup chopped beef suet, one cup molasses, one do. warm milk, one do. stoned raisins, one cup and a half flour, one teaspoon soda, cinnamon, cloves, and nutmeg, a little of each. Butter the dish, and steam four hours.

BISCUIT

One quart milk, one tablespoon sugar, two do. butter, a little salt, three eggs, half cup yeast; have the milk as warm as the hand can bear. Stir quite stiff with flour.

LEMON PIE

The grated rind and juice of one lemon, one cup powdered sugar, yelks of three eggs, two tablespoons flour, 3-4ths of a cup of water. Take the whites of the eggs and three tablespoons sugar, beat to a stiff froth, and turn it over the pie. When baked, set it in the oven again and brown it. Use but one crust.

CREAM PUFF

Two cups flour, one do. butter, half pint water; boil the butter and water together; stir in the flour by degrees while boiling; cool it, then add five eggs and one-fourth of a teaspoon of soda. Drop on buttered tins, and bake in a quick oven. Dressing—One pint milk, one cup sugar, two eggs, half cup flour; beat the eggs, sugar, and flour together; stir them in the milk while boiling; flavor with vanilla. Break the cakes half round and fill with the cream, which should be made first. Do not beat the eggs for the cake or for the cream. This quantity makes about fifty.

MISS MADISON'S WHIM

Two pounds flour, two do. sugar, one and a half do. butter, 12 eggs, one wine-glass brandy, two nutmegs and a half, one teaspoon soda, two pounds stoned raisins.

SWEET PICKLES

Seven lbs tomatoes, four lbs sugar, one ounce cloves, two do. cinnamon, one quart vinegar. Pour the vinegar, with the spices and sugar, boiling hot over the fruit, three mornings in succession, then cook the fruit thoroughly; take it out, and boil the syrup as much as you like.

DELMONICO PUDDING

One quart milk, three tablespoons corn starch; stir it in the milk just before boiling; boil three minutes; take yelks of five eggs and six tablespoons sugar; pour milk and starch on the eggs and sugar, flavor and salt. Pour it into the dish you wish to serve it in, and bake long enough to hold the iceing. Beat the whites of the eggs with three tablespoons sugar, lay it over the pudding, set in the oven, and brown a little.

CREAM SPONGE

Two eggs, one cup sugar; break the eggs in a cup, fill the cup with sweet cream, beat both together, one teaspoon soda, two do. cream tartar, rub cream tartar in the flour.

GINGER SNAPS

Two cups sugar, two do. molasses, one cup and a half butter, one tablespoon ginger, one do. soda, one teaspoon cloves, two do. cinnamon, one cup sour milk, flour enough to make up.

BEEF SUET PUDDING

Take suet, pick out all the strings and skin, then chop it very fine, mix with flour, season with pepper, salt, summer savory, sage, and sweet margery. Dress the inwards of the beef or of a pig as you would for sausage. Stuff them, and boil slowly nearly an hour, occasionally pricking them with a fork. When done, hang them up to dry; they are then ready for use at all seasons. Boil them over to warm when you wish to eat them.

CHICKEN SALAD

Boil two or three chickens; when cold, slice off all the white meat, chop it fine, chop celery enough to season it well, mustard and black pepper to your taste; add strong vinegar, and the yelks of three eggs boiled hard and rubbed to a cream.

CHICKEN PIE

Stew and season your chicken well. Bake a rich flaky pastry, lay it on a large platter, split the pastry in small pieces, laying between them the chicken and dressing.

INDIAN MEAL PUDDING

Into one quart of boiling milk stir one quart sifted meal; then add one quart cold milk, two well-beaten eggs, half teacup sugar, one do. flour, salt and spice to taste; stir it well, and pour into a buttered dish; bake two hours; serve with butter.

STEAMED INDIAN PUDDING

One pint sour milk, one do. sweet milk, one tablespoon sour cream; stir in Indian meal to make a thick batter; add one teaspoon soda, one do. salt; steam three hours; serve with sweetened cream. A handful of fruit, fresh or dried, stirred in, will be an addition.

CARROT PUDDING

One lb flour, half lb potatoes, half lb suet, quarter lb sugar, half lb carrots; chop the suet, carrots, and potatoes; mix all well; add raisins and currants; boil three or four hours.

MRS. H.'S PUDDING

One pint sweet milk, one teaspoon soda, half cup molasses, two cups Indian meal, one cup flour; steam two hours.

BOILED PLUM PUDDING

Take one lb suet chopped; add one lb currants, one lb stoned raisins, one lb flour, one pint milk, eight eggs, and one nutmeg; beat the eggs well; mix thoroughly; boil four or five hours.

POTATO PUDDING

Two lbs potatoes boiled and mashed, half lb sugar, half lb butter, six eggs, one wine-glass brandy, and one nutmeg; line a dish with paste, and bake.

EVE'S PUDDING

Six ounces grated bread, six or seven chopped apples, six ounces sugar, six do. currants, six eggs, nutmeg to taste, six ounces suet chopped; boil three hours.

MALINDA RUSSELL

KATE'S PUDDING

One quart flour, two teaspoons cream tartar, one do. soda, one lb chopped suet, half lb currants, half lb raisins; mix with cold water to a thick batter; boil two hours; eat with sauce.

KENTUCKY PUDDING

One cup and a half sugar, one cup butter, five eggs, one teaspoon soda, two do cream tartar, one cup milk, three do flour; bake in a quick oven forty-five minutes.

COOKIES

One cup butter, one do. sweet milk, two do. sugar, two teaspoons cream tartar, one do. soda, flour to roll; roll thin, cut in small cakes; bake twenty minutes; any seed you choose.

SUGAR SNAPS

One cup butter, two do. sugar, three eggs, one teaspoon soda, one tablespoon ginger, flour to roll; bake quick.

APPLE FLOAT

Whites of two beaten eggs; add a spoonful of sugar, six apples stewed and drained until quite dry; beat all together, then make a soft custard, put in the bottom of a dish, lay the float on top of it.

DRIED APPLE PUDDING

Chop dried apples, wash and rub dry in flour; stir into a batter, and boil in a bag; eat with butter sauce.

BLANC MANGE

To two ounces of gelatine put three pints rich milk, flavor with lemon or vanilla, sweeten with white sugar. Put all on the fire cold, and stir frequently till all dissolve. Strain it, and when partially cool, pour into your moulds.

A-LA-MODE BEEF

Take a round of beef, make a great many holes through it, roll strips of raw salt pork in a seasoning of one half teaspoon each of thyme, salt, pepper; and cloves. Draw through the holes these strips of pork. Put six onions, two tablespoons milk, and one quarter lb butter in a saucepan, stew them tender, put all into a pot, with water enough to cover them; let it cook slowly five hours. Before taking up, add a pint of claret wine if you choose.

POTTED BEEF

Take a beef shank, put it in water sufficient to cover it; boil till tender; remove the bone and cartilage; chop the meat fine, and put back into the kettle with the liquor, which should be one quart; simmer gently; season with salt, pepper, and mace to suit the taste. When cool, cut it in slices, to be passed around like dried beef. Potted beef can be kept any length of time by chopping fine, seasoning high, and packing hard in a stone jar, setting it in a cool place and covering closely.

PRESSED BEEF

Sew tightly in a bag a round of beef, first sticking it full of cloves and pepper. When about half-done, throw into the water a handful of cloves, with salt, pepper, and mustard. When cold, take off the cloth, slice thin, and eat cold for tea.

BEST WAY TO ROAST BEEF

Wash in warm water your beef, then rub in salt and pepper, and dry flour until a moisture rises on the meat; put it into a dripping-pan, setting it on a brick in the oven, keeping the bottom simmering, the top with a quick heat, turning the roast often till done. The juice that flows from the meat will cook it always sweet and tender.

FORCED STEAK

Grind the steak through the mill, then put it out into rolls; put into a saucepan one tablespoon lard, seasoning the steak with pepper and salt; add a very little water. Simmer until done, turning often; chop onions fine, laying over the meat; baste the meat with the liquid and onions. When done, make a butter and cream gravy, and serve hot.

TURKEY POT PIE

Cut the turkey into small pieces, and boil until done. Paste the dripping-pan with rich pastry, lay on the meat, cut small strips of dough, lay it among the meat, season with pepper and butter; turn the gravy into the pan and cover with crust, cutting a place in the top, and bake moderately.

MALINDA RUSSELL

CALF HEAD SOUP

Dress the head and boil until done, remove the bones from the meat, take all the meat from the upper part of the head and chop fine, and put it into the soup, with chopped potatoes and carrots, shives, pepper, salt, parsley, sweet margery, and a little butter. Stir a little flour and milk together to thicken the soup. Make a hash of the meat from the under jaw. Take the brains from the head, beat up eggs as for an omelet, turn this over the brains after seasoning with salt and pepper. Melt some butter and turn on. Set it in the oven to cook slowly. Skin and slice the tongue; put into a saucepan, with butter, pepper, and salt. Stew dry.

TO BOIL AND DRESS MUTTON HAM

Perforate the ham, and put slices of onion in. Rub it with salt. Canvas the ham, put in whole grains of pepper and cloves; sew it tight, and boil until done. Take three spoons sugar, one half pint Madeira wine, butter, thicken with flour; boil and turn it over the ham with parsley.

TO COOK PARSNIPS

Pare the parsnips and put them into a bag, season with salt, boil until done. When cold, slice, roll them in flour, and pepper them. Brown them in lard, and turn drawn butter over them.

TO COOK IRISH POTATOES

Pare and boil quickly; when done, turn into a colander. Mash them and dress with cream, butter, pepper and salt, pat them out into cakes and bake them. A good way is to put in the yelks of two or three eggs, and boiled codfish picked up fine, made into balls with the potato, buttered and baked.

HOW TO COOK AND DRESS OCHER

Boil in clear water or with vegetables; when tender, drain off the water; dress it with butter, pepper and salt, and let it simmer or fry.

VEGETABLE OYSTERS

Scrape and boil tender; mash them, dress them with butter, salt and pepper. Pat them out and bake brown.

MALINDA RUSSELL

BEEF SOUP

Take the shank bone, boil until tender; chop fine, potatoes, onions, and cabbage, and boil until done; season with salt, pepper, parsley, rosemary, or sweet margery. Rub the yelk of one egg into three tablespoons flour, rubbed into rolls and dropped into the soup to boil.

CHICKEN SOUP

Boil one or two chickens whole with half a pint of rice until tender. Take out the chickens; make a batter of sour milk, two or three eggs, a little soda, with flour; drop this into the soup in spoonfuls; pepper and salt to taste. To dress the chickens, drawn butter and pepper. Boil three or four eggs hard and slice them, laying them over the chicken, with gell, sprigs of parsley.

HOW TO BOIL FISH

Take pickerel, salmon, buffalo, or red horse; rub them with a little saltpetre mixed with salt; put inside the fish whole grains of pepper; sew them up tight in a cloth and boil three hours. When done, turn them into a large platter; dress with drawn butter and chopped parsley or rosemary.

FRICASEED CATFISH

Boil in water with a little salt until done, then drain off the water, and turn over the fish rich cream, butter, pepper, and a little flour, and simmer slowly.

HAM OMELET

Fry the ham about two minutes into a little hot fat, beat the eggs, season with salt and pepper; mix a little flour and water into a batter, and stir into the eggs; turn this over the ham, and turn quickly.

RICE OMELET

Pat out into thin cakes cold boiled rice, beat the eggs and season, then drop the cakes into the egg, fry quickly, and turn into a platter and butter them.

FRIED OYSTERS

Let the oysters stand in vinegar while you prepare a batter of eggs or milk and flour; season the batter to your taste; drop the oysters into the batter, and fry in butter or lard.

MALINDA RUSSELL

PICKLED ROAST PIG

Dress and stuff your pig, put it into a dripping-pan and put it baking; take one pint of strong vinegar, Madeira wine, or currant wine, put into a basin with half lb butter; boil together; stir in a little batter made of flour and water; baste the meat with this quite often until done.

MAGNETIC OIL

One ounce chloroform, one do. laudanum, one do. tincture of colchicum, one do. capsicum, half do. castor oil, three do. alcohol.

BLACK OINTMENT

One ounce red lead, one do. sweet oil, one do. linseed oil.

PELEG WHITE STICKING SALVE

Seven pounds rosin, one pound beeswax, one pound mutton suet, two ounces gum arabic.

BARBERS' SHAMPOOING MIXTURE

One pint soft water, one ounce sal soda, half ounce cream tartar. Applying a few spoonfuls, rub the roots of the hair thoroughly; use a little warm water at the same time; then wash well from the head and apply a little oil. This should be done once a week.

BARBERS' STAR HAIR OIL

Castor oil six and a half pints, alcohol one pint and a half, citronella and lavender oil half ounce each, mixed and well shaken.

COLOGNE

Take oil rosemary and lemon each 1-4th oz., oil begamot and lavender each 1-8th oz., oil cinnamon eight drops, oils clove and rose fifteen drops, alcohol two quarts. Mix and shake well two or three times a day for a week.

TO CURE CORNS

Soak the feet fifteen or twenty minutes, night and morning, in cool water; remove at each time all which can be removed, without pain or bleeding; keep away all pressure.

MALINDA RUSSELL

DENTIFRICE

Dentifrice removes tartarous adhesions, and induces a healthy action of the gums. Dissolve one ounce borax in one pint and a half boiling water; when cool, add one teaspoonful tincture of myrrh and one tablespoonful of the spirits of camphor, and bottle for use. Take a tablespoonful of the mixture to the same amount of warm water, and apply at bed-time with a soft brush; a stiff bristle brush should never be used, as they injure the gums.

BURNS

After applying sweet oil, scrape the inside of a raw potato, lay it on the burn. In a short time put on fresh potato; repeat it quite often; it draws out the fire and gives immediate relief.

TOOTHACHE

Alum reduced to powder two drachms, nitrous spirits of ether seven drachms; mix and apply to the tooth; this is a certain cure. Or put into the tooth a pill made of camphor and opium.

RESTORING THE HAIR TO ITS ORIGINAL COLOR

Lac Sulphuris two drachms, rose water eight ounces. Shake it thoroughly, and apply every night before going to bed.

CURE FOR RHEUMATISM

One lb sarsaparilla, one do. prickly ash bark, one do. cherry bark off the root, one do. bittersweet root, half lb sweet fern, half lb wintergreen. Boil down to one gallon, and add one quart rum. Dose—one tablespoonful three times a day.

MAGIC OIL

One ounce laudanum, one ounce chloroform, half ounce oil of sassafras, one ounce oil of hemlock, half ounce Cayenne pepper, one ounce oil cedar, half ounce camphor gum; add two quarts alcohol.

ELIXIR PAREGORIC

Opium three drachms, licorice ball 3-4ths ounce or six drachms, gum camphor three scruples or 1-8th ounce, oil anise two drachms or 1-4th ounce. Bruise opium and licorice fine, put it into half pint boiling water, and steep until thoroughly dissolved; put it into a bottle, add the oil anise, benzoin and camphor. Shake thoroughly several times in the course of twenty or thirty hours. It will then be fit for use.

CURE FOR CORNS

Four ounces potash, two drops oil vitriol, one tablespoon alum pulverized.

CURE FOR DROPSY

Queen of the Meadow steeped in water without washing the roots.

GINGER POP BEER

Five and a half gallons water, 3-4ths lb ginger root bruised, half ounce tartaric acid, two and 3-4ths lbs white sugar, whites of three eggs well beaten, one teaspoonful lemon oil, one gill yeast. Boil the root thirty minutes in one gallon of water. Strain off and put the oil in while hot. Make over night; in the morning skim and bottle, keeping out the sediment.

ICE CREAM

Half lb loaf sugar to a quart of cream or milk, boil a soft custard, six eggs to one quart of milk; eggs to be beaten.

Another is made as follows:

Boil one quart of milk; stir into it, while boiling, one tablespoon arrow-root; wet with cold milk; when cool, stir in the yelk of an egg to give a rich color; five minutes is enough to boil. In either receipt put in the sugar after they cool; keep the same proportions for any amount. The juice of strawberries or raspberries gives a color and flavor to ice creams—one ounce of extract to a gallon. Break the ice well, one quart salt to one pail ice. Half hour stirring and scraping down will freeze it.

TO PRESERVE MILK

Put a spoonful of horse radish into a pan of milk, and it can be kept sweet for several days.

TO PRESERVE EGGS

Eggs can be kept good for months by this preparation: one pint of coarse salt and one pint of unslacked lime in a pail of water. Keep cool.

MALINDA RUSSELL